This book was created to educate children on butterfly habitat requirements. I encourage you to research the native butterflies in your area and how you can build strong habitats for them to thrive in.

Author and creator: Della Wilder

This butterfly is looking for a new home and they need your help!

Their home needs to protect them
from the wind and the rain

Fences, vines, shrubs, and trees can all help protect them from the wind and rain! Do you see a spot this butterfly can use as a home?

Butterflies need native flowering plants for food. Butterflies are attracted to flowers in red, yellow, orange, pink, and purple. Do you spot any flowers for this butterfly?

Butterflies enjoy the warmth of the sun! A good butterfly home must have some sunshine.

Does this spot look like a warm and sunny place for our butterfly?

When butterflies are not taking shelter or
enjoying the warmth from the sun, they
need room to spread their wings and fly!

Is there room here for our
butterfly to soar through the sky?

Butterflies need our help to give them a place to live. This tree house has lots of options for our butterfly to live around it! Can you spot one?

Our butterfly is getting hungry! Lets find some flowers with sweet nectar for them to eat.

Our butterfly has found a field of yummy flowers! What color flowers do you see?

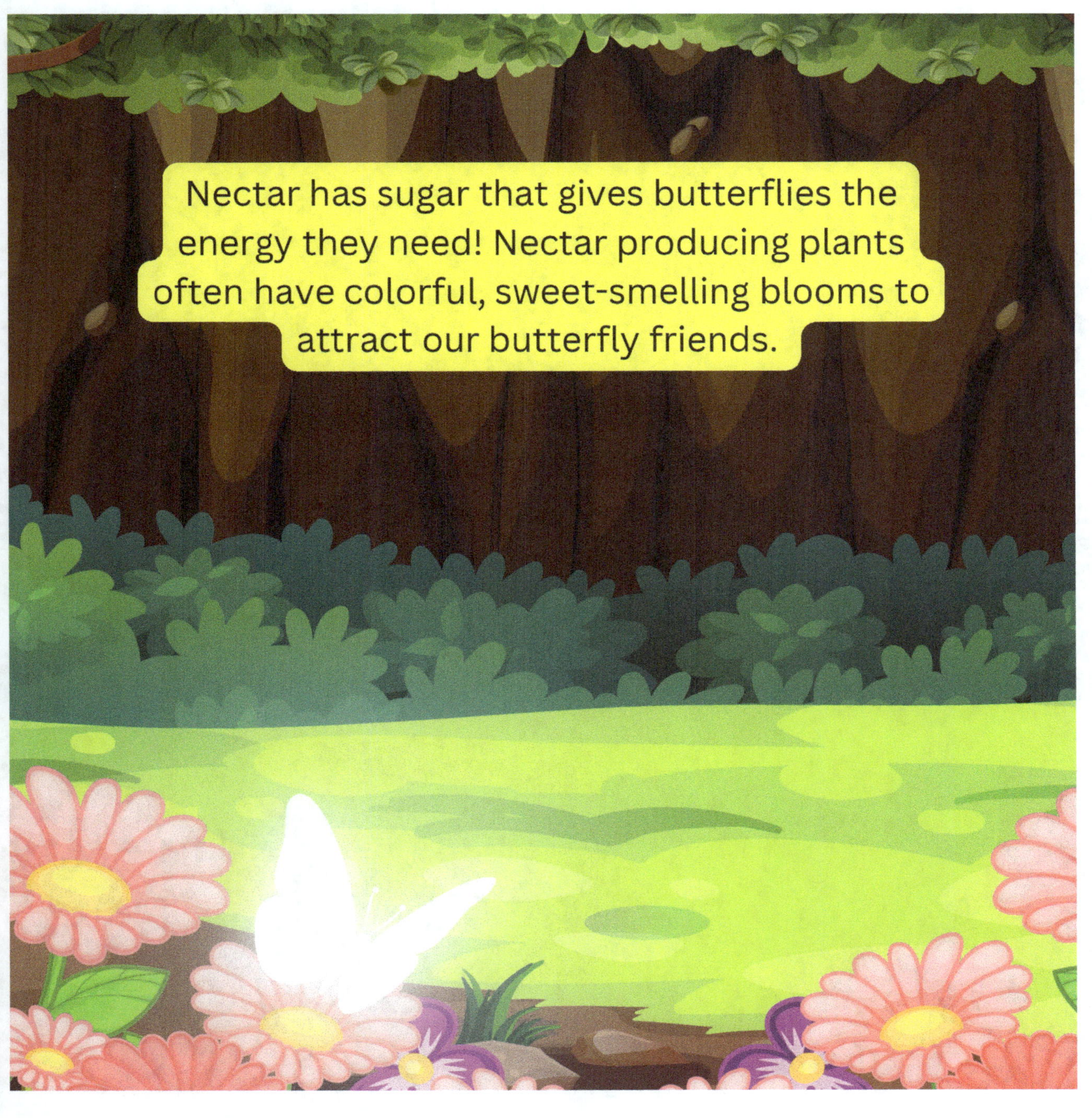

Nectar has sugar that gives butterflies the energy they need! Nectar producing plants often have colorful, sweet-smelling blooms to attract our butterfly friends.

Now that our butterfly friend has a tummy full of nectar, they are ready to burn off that energy and fly!

Butterflies can fly between 50 to 100 miles in one day!

After a long day of flying, butterflies need to rest, but they don't sleep!

When a butterfly is resting its called,
"roosting". Butterflies often hang upside
down from leaves or twigs in trees.

Can you spot a place for our butterfly to roost?

Our butterfly has found the perfect place to rest! Do you see any flowers they can enjoy after they have finished resting?

Now that our butterfly is rested and had a snack, they are ready to fly!

Thank you for helping us find the perfect habitat for our butterfly friend! There are lots of places to play, take shelter, find food, and warm up in the sun!

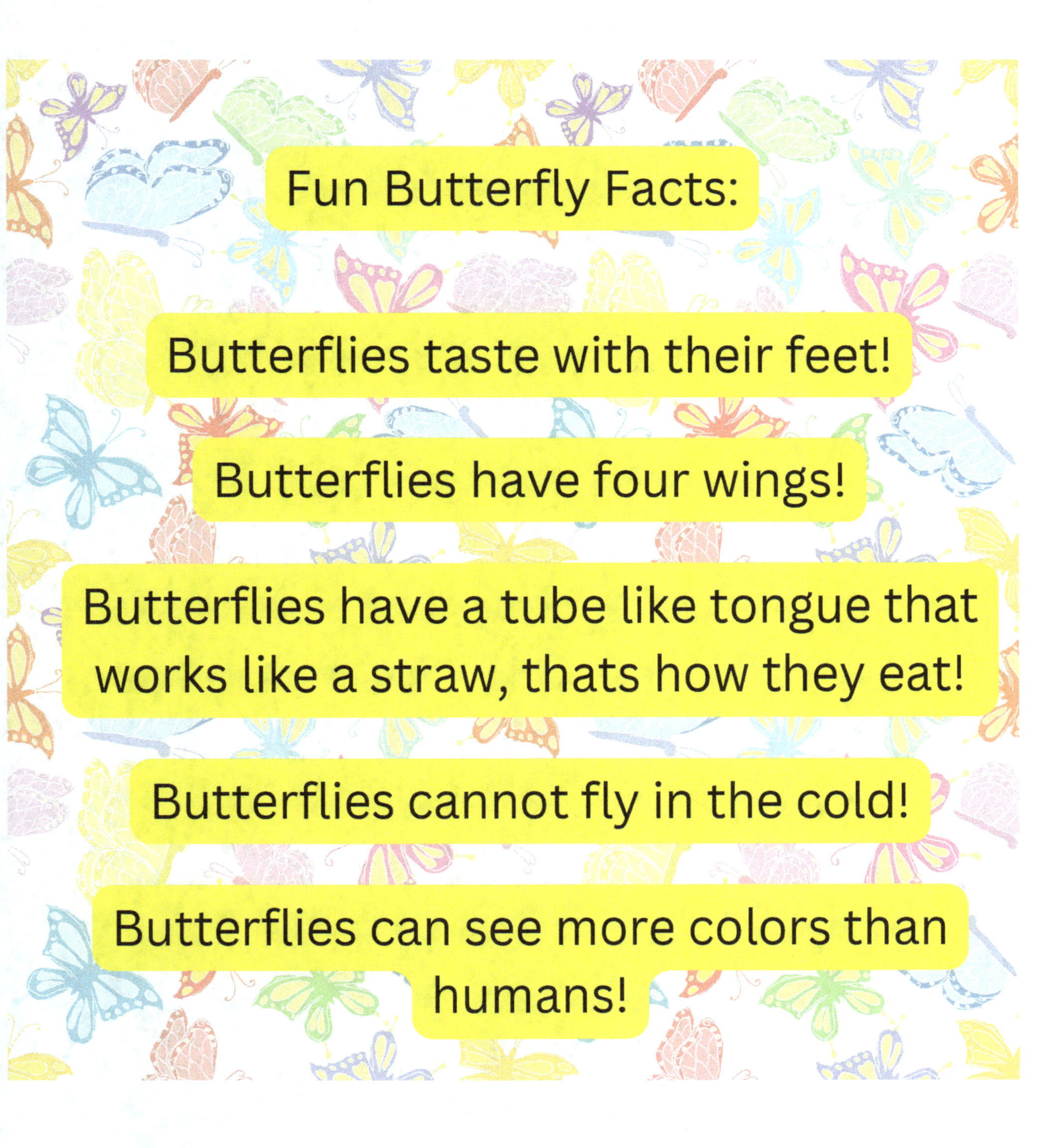

Fun Butterfly Facts:

Butterflies taste with their feet!

Butterflies have four wings!

Butterflies have a tube like tongue that works like a straw, thats how they eat!

Butterflies cannot fly in the cold!

Butterflies can see more colors than humans!

Butterflies come in a wide variety and have different habitat needs! Some butterflies can live and feed on many plants while others may require certain kinds. You can research the butterflies native to your area and become a butterfly ally!